D0116276

What Can She Be?
A MUSICIAN

What Can She Be?
A MUSICIAN

Gloria and Esther Goldreich
photographs by Robert Ipcar

Lothrop, Lee & Shepard Company • New York

The authors wish to thank
Bill Sonnenberg, the Electric Lady Recording Studio
and the Manhattan School of Music
for their cooperation.

Photographs on page 20 and top of page 21 by William Diament.

Text copyright © 1975 by Gloria Goldreich and Esther Goldreich
Photographs copyright © 1975 by Robert Ipcar

Printed in the United States of America.

2   3   4   5

Library of Congress Cataloging in Publication Data

Goldreich, Gloria.
  What can she be?

  SUMMARY: Introduces the varied aspects of a career in music through a description of the daily activities of a female musician who composes, performs, teaches, and conducts music.
  1. Music as a profession—Juvenile literature. 2. Women musicians—Juvenile literature. [1. Music as a profession. 2. Vocational guidance] I. Goldreich, Esther, joint author. II. Ipcar, Robert, ill. III. Title.
ML3930.A2G64   780'.23   74-28461
ISBN 0-688-41701-9
ISBN 0-688-51701-3 lib. bdg.

This is Leslie Pearl. Leslie is a musician. She plays many musical instruments, like the piano, the guitar, and the harpsichord. She also writes music and lyrics, the words to her new songs. Leslie teaches grown-ups and children how to play instruments. She wants many people to know the joy of making music and of putting sounds together into beautiful arrangements.

Leslie begins her day very early because she has so much to do. Her first stop is at Karen's house. She will give Karen a piano lesson.

Karen is seven years old. When Leslie was Karen's age, she took piano lessons too. She learned that playing an instrument

8

can be very hard work. She sometimes practiced two hours a day. But Leslie didn't mind working hard because she loved playing the piano so much.

Leslie took music lessons for many years. She went to a music college where she studied many different instruments. She also learned about composing music and how to conduct an orchestra. She studied harmony and theory, which teaches how musical ideas can be expressed.

Leslie explains this to Karen who listens carefully. Karen is very proud. Today she will start to practice a piece that Leslie has composed. Karen begins practicing as Leslie rushes off to her next lesson.

Natalie has been studying piano for many years. She is always glad when Leslie works with her on a new piece. When her lesson is over, she asks Leslie if she has composed any new songs.

Leslie plays her new song "Jonathan's Home Again." She

12

tells Natalie that she wrote this song for her sister Debbie, who is a singer. Natalie thinks the song is lovely. She plays it on the piano while Leslie sings and plays the bass guitar.

Leslie meets Debbie to rehearse the new song. Leslie explains that she wrote it for Debbie's voice. Some singers have high sweet voices and some singers have strong low voices. When composers write songs for a particular singer, they think of the kind of voice the singer has. They try to write music that will go well with that voice.

14

Debbie has a strong voice and she loves to sing songs that tell a story. "Jonathan's Home Again" is that kind of song. It tells the story of a friend who has just come home after a long time.

The mood of the music must fit the song's words. Leslie tried out many different melodies. Finally she found a melody that seemed right for the lyrics. She chose the chords she needed to go along with this melody.

Next Leslie wrote out the melody and the chords on musical composition paper in the special language of music. Musicians read music just as other people read books. Each note has a meaning for them and tells them what sound to play or sing.

Now Leslie tries the melody with other instruments, such as the cello and the guitar, to see how the song sounds. Debbie reads the music and the lyrics. She writes herself reminders so that she will know when to sing loudly and when her voice must be soft. Debbie sings as Leslie plays.

Debbie and Leslie test the new song at a neighborhood coffee house. The audience loves it. People clap so hard that the sisters sing and play it once more. It looks as if "Jonathan's Home Again" will be a hit song, the kind of song people want to hear again and again.

Leslie meets a group of musicians for lunch. They talk about
all the things that are happening in the music world. One
musician is looking for someone to play the piano for a recording. Leslie says she will be glad to do it. A trombonist

invites everyone to a jazz concert that night. Leslie's friend Edna, who plays the oboe with a symphony orchestra, has two extra tickets for a concert.

Musicians are always busy—playing their instruments, listening to all kinds of music, and planning for new recordings and performances.

Leslie must rush to her next job. She has written the music and words for a radio commercial about cameras. A few days ago a group of musicians recorded the background music for this commercial.

Each instrument was recorded on a separate track on the tape. Now the sound engineer blends all the tracks together to make the best sound.

22

Leslie is also the producer of the commercial. She works
with the sound engineer and decides how loud or how soft
each instrument should sound. She also knows that the commercial must be exactly one minute long. That is all the time
they will have on the radio.

The music is three seconds too long. The engineer follows Leslie's instructions and cuts the tape. Now the problem is solved.

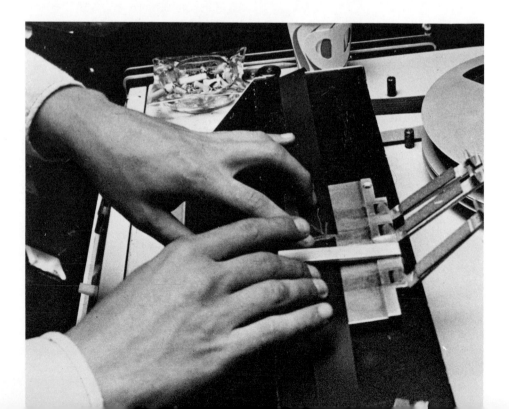

Debbie arrives at the recording studio. Leslie and Debbie sing the lively little song Leslie has written. It tells people what clear pictures the camera can take of indoor birthday parties and outdoor picnics.

As they sing "Picnics and Parties," the sound engineer records their voices. Then he blends this voice track with the tracks of the background music. Leslie listens closely. The whole tape sounds just right and everyone is pleased.

Leslie has fun working on commercials, but she is glad to get home to work on her own song "Jonathan's Home Again." On a sheet of musical composition paper, she writes out the basic melody line, the lyrics, and the chords. This is called the "lead sheet."

Leslie sends the lead sheet to the Library of Congress in Washington, D.C. She will get it back with a government stamp or seal. This means the song belongs to Leslie.

Photograph © 1973 Silver Blue Music, New York.

Leslie is always pleased when she has a chance to conduct music. A conductor helps musicians to work together, chooses the music to be played, and beats time for the orchestra. The conductor also decides how each piece of music should sound —when it should be slow or fast, loud or soft.

When Leslie waves her baton toward the violinists, they know it is time for them to play. When her baton slams downward, the pianist knows he must play the notes that tell the listener a storm is brewing.

The baton has its own language. Good conductors use this language to tell the musicians how they want the music to sound.

One of the things Leslie loves about her work is that almost every day something new and different is happening. Today she is playing with other musicians in a concert. At this performance she will play both the piano and the cello.

Not all musicians can play more than one instrument. Because she knows how to play many instruments, Leslie knows

how they will sound when they are played together. This helps her when she composes music and when she works out new ways of playing old songs. She knows which instruments should be used to express ideas and feelings. The light sweet

notes of a violin might be used to give the idea of a spring day. The heavy crashing notes of the lower piano keyboard can tell the listener it is winter.

The audience at the concert loves the music. They applaud the musicians and call, "More! More! Encore!"

Today Leslie is very excited. The Library of Congress has sent back her lead sheet with the government seal. Now she telephones Eddie Brown, her manager.

35

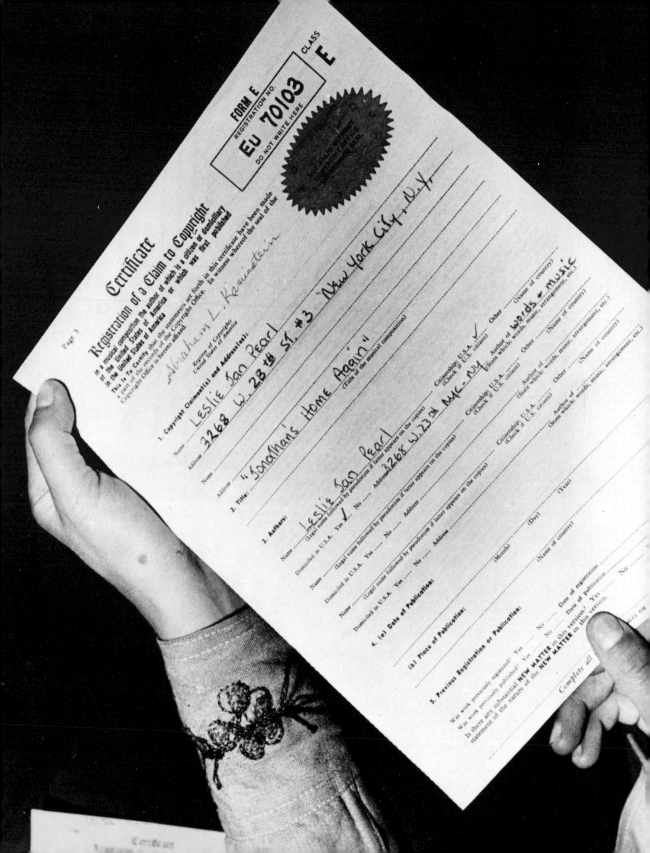

A musician's manager arranges all the business details. He discusses how much money a musician should be paid for each job. He meets with record companies to work out how much they will pay for new songs. It is his job to sell Leslie's work. This gives Leslie more time for her music.

Eddie Brown likes "Jonathan's Home Again." He tells her to go ahead and make a tape recording. Then he will try to sell the song to a record company.

Leslie chooses the musicians who will play their instruments as Debbie sings. It is important to find good musicians who work well together. She rents a recording studio where they work on the song. Fred, the drummer, is playing his part too fast. Leslie asks him to play more slowly. Tom, the guitarist, wants to change some notes at the end. Leslie agrees with his idea and makes the change. She asks Debbie to sing more softly in one place.

After many rehearsals and some changes in the chords, Leslie thinks the song is ready to record. She works with the sound engineers as the music is captured on tape. The musicians record the song again and again until it is perfect. Finally, Leslie gives Eddie Brown the finished tape.

A big record company decides to buy Leslie's song. Eddie
Brown arranges a contract, an agreement between Leslie and
the record company. Leslie will let the company record her
song. Then every time someone buys the record, the company
will pay part of the money to Leslie. The record company
also makes a contract with Debbie, who will sing the song.

42

Leslie's song will be copied on thousands of records. A special kind of needle cuts grooves into a blank record and the sound is engraved in these grooves. When a phonograph needle touches the grooves, it picks up the sound just as a magnet picks up a metal object.

Leslie can hardly wait to play the first record of "Jonathan's Home Again." The record company will send copies of the record to disc jockeys at many radio stations all over the

country. Disc jockeys play many records on their shows. Soon listeners in Maine and California, Iowa and Arkansas, New York and Florida will know the melody and the words to "Jonathan's Home Again." Some of them may like the song so much that they will buy the record. It gives Leslie, her sister Debbie, and all the musicians who worked on the recording a good feeling to know that so many people will hear their music.

Leslie is often tired at the end of a busy day, but she is never too tired for music. Some evenings she listens to records from her collection. Sometimes she practices one of her instruments

while her pets listen. But what she likes best is a jam session with her musician friends. Together they play music for their own pleasure far into the night.

Leslie loves being a musician. She enjoys creating music and sharing her knowledge and love of music with others. Leslie thinks that working with music and musicians is the very best kind of work for her to do.